Holy Trinity
Maiden Mother Crone

Tess Galati

Dedicated to every child who reaches for the moon.

If evolution is the goal, and I believe it is,
the only question that matters is, *what's next?!*

Contents

Crone

Reconciliation

Acknowledgments

"In the Pediatric Ward" appeared in *Pulse: Voices from the Heart of Medicine, More Voices—a second anthology,* 2012, editors Paul Gross M.D. and Diane Guernsey.

"Holy Trinity: Maiden, Mother, Crone" appeared in *13th Moon, A Feminist Literary Magazine,* Volume 18, 2002.

Maiden

Spring: Bonsai and Grace

Scrub elms on the rocky banks of Lake Superior bend against the uncompromising wind. Along the Peloponnesian coast, bay laurels, cramped and thickened, force a path through rocky crags seeking unsalted water. In California's desert, Joshua trees sacrifice leaves and branches, becoming a bulbous scaffolding to catch the rain. Growth threatened is tentative, strategic.

Branches of stressed bonsai survivors—distorted, stylized, wonderfully limned—comfort those threatened by war, controlled by addiction, short of attention, bereft of love. Like us, they grow strategically, turning energy to present need. They plant their seedlings where they can, and hope the dowry of their DNA suffices for the growing. Some seedlings surrender to the sea, the wind. A few cling to earth. They grow into a tree family, a family tree, shaped by stress. Some call such families dysfunctional. I call us distinctive.

Hothouse trees, fed and watered, grow simple, lush, uncompli-cated, balanced as a pendulum. Their scaffolds are straightforward, easily known—ideal growth without struggle. Their splendor is un-equivocal, but it leaves me cold and restless.

I love those trees that stand resplendent in their multifaceted, teeming specificity, their burgeoning differentness. I cherish stands of trees that do not lack for stress. I honor families emerging from hunger, sickness, anger, stupidity, dearth of love. Persisting nonetheless, they are as different from one another as are the leaves of apple trees from pines.

I have read that Jesus was a man made in just such a distinctive family: illegitimate son of a carpenter and a simple woman, his parents refugees from murderous hordes, born in the soiled straw where animals fed. I have learned that He was the legitimate child of God, like you and me and the triumphant oak in my garden.

We who have grown in distinctive families cannot be pinned down. We own our totem, our relentless force of growth. We carry the coded messages of our ancestors' stress. We are the bonsai people, ready for new planting.

Meraki: Camp Canweta

Meraki is the Greek term for the essence of self that's instilled into objects when one loves the making of them.

Leftover corn in the fields
Shrapnel of Iowa winter
Mopwater smear of sky

A convoy of faded moms
Lipsticked, gloved and sweatered
Encased in Buicks and Chevys
Crawls toward Camp Canweta
For Campfire Girl Spring Cleaning.

In the back seat, a jumble of girls
Jumble of tools in the trunk
Shredded sponges, torn towels
Rags stained and wadded.

Squeezed between blondes, I cradle
A package—brown paper, string tied:
Mother's gift-wrapped meraki.

Because we are not like them, she mumbled
Measuring perfect squares
Cut from threadbare bedsheets,
Bleached, creased twice, double ironed.

Blondes gasp and giggle
As my unwrapped rags take wing
Float and fall, parachuted:
Folios of love, love follies.

Wealth

That whole Iowa winter
while Mother worked at the factory,
Dad at the town hotel,
and we kids went to school,
Aunt Sofia from the old country
raised the thermostat,
opened windows,
hung bedsheets over the sills
to catch scarce sun.

Alone all day, she taught
the parakeet greetings in Greek.
His chatter at night was ceaseless.
She saved every jar and bottle—
mayonnaise, honey, oil,
olive, pickle, jam—
a clutter in every cupboard.

Thus she described America:
A practical land, cold,
lacking in sun and culture,
but rich in jars and bottles.

When she left, we gained
more shelf space
lower heating bills
silence (the parakeet went mute)
And our bedsheets never again
smelled so sweet.

Memorial Day: Ames, Iowa

Ragtag Legionnaires,
crimson and gold braid strewn
across capacious bellies,
shoulder rifles down Main Street
to municipal graves of mostly
shopkeepers, teachers, bankers:
gentry of small town Iowa.

We kids, in a knot, wait
through *'valor our country we gather,*
not in vain on this now died for,'
poised to pounce on the graves,
retrieve spent bullet shells
after the ritual firing.

Later, while moms lay out flowers
we circle a grave to count
our bounty:
bullets
drawn blank

for this

memorial

killing.

1942–1962

You tell me of
bodies shoveled
ten deep in this green valley,
a toddler
shot for crossing their line.

You say
I cried
for milk at your empty breast.
You gave
pints of blood for grams of flour.
Brave in the night,
starving, you rocked me to sleep
at your breast.

You saw
a neighbor
scratch through corpses for gold;
a young girl
raped on our street and then shot;
a soldier
turning to kill an old woman.

How can you see
the hungers in
this plump land,
this idle foreignness,
the
wandering
depression.

This is
their agony.
Their agony and mine.
Incomprehensible.

On Hearing of the Execution of Alekos Panagoulis

Alekos Panagoulis was executed in Athens during the period of the Greek dictatorship that lasted from April 21, 1967, until November 17, 1974. Word of Alekos's execution traveled to a small band of expatriate resistance fighters in Minneapolis, Minnesota.

So start the dance.

It was a long enough night
Keeping the watchman's count
Of fresh graves marking the roads.

Our people, beached in their sorrow,
Curse the rocky homeland,
The hungry, tearful mother.

We sing our measured song.

In this land we reside as strangers.
Packed in ships like fodder,
We've disowned our feet and hands:
Tools in the strange agora.

Papers, tags, numbers,
Render us proper citizens.
Socrates, too, is young
When he loses the taste for garlic.

So start the dance.

Paper the tags with rhythms
While our eloquent sons and lovers
Paint music under our feet.

With the cargo we sneak in relics
Under our tongues: the songs.

Minutes for the Final Meeting of the Committee to Construct a Model of the Human Condition (CCMHC)

Oh you make it so easy
with your active values listening
clarification releaser skills oh.

Give me a name tag and I
will write on it the end of your
forced choice continuum.

Give me twenty questions and
I'll give you twenty questions and
we'll resolve our conflicts and
(do I remind you of your druthers?) and
little upsets (murders) and
news and
goods and
discharges (wow) and
detonations and
reflections and

hi.

My name is Jezebel: I love to dance and screw.
My name is Ishmael: I touched bottom once but was saved by a coffin.
My name is Odysseus: I am the black sea beating against your sides.
My name is Dashi: I have nothing to tell you.
My name is Pumpkin Pie: I was born as a joke.

My name is your name went to school East North South
Roosevelt West High when my parents didn't
know didn't mean to
know didn't have two three one no
brothers sisters didn't
how can I tell
you didn't ask didn't

know didn't
mean to know didn't
have a space for that one.

We are not asking questions
not—careful—not breaking hearts
not wanting any more
looking down our throats
regrets not
sad not
sorry.

I'm so sorry.

We are passing time making noises models
while we die are dying are
every day, let us say, in our own
foolish way dying alone.

Let me comfort you, just once, with
this, I'm afraid, rotting bunch of grapes
lick your wounds,
you whom I love because
(mark this: there is no other reason)
you are, like me,
a dying animal.

Encounters

I.
Word is a fragile thing.
Just silence quivers with lies.

Word spins a spider web.
It sticks to the skin that dies.

So tentative, we drop
a heavy pearl that must
pull down the wispy threads
leave them a heap of dust.

II.
I am the wildebeest, the running flanks.

The antelope stirs in your hair
blooms in the crook of your arm.

My palm is the tiger's lair.
Laughter's a clutch of sparrows.

In the corner of the eye
a sleeping butterfly shudders
        begins to fly.

My Left Hand Hardly Knows What My Right Hand Is Doing and Vice Versa

It is always slinking away,
painting its fingernails fuchsia,
digging up roots in the garden,
snapping and crackling all night:
It's become a general nuisance.
It tore away its glove
and hopped a freight headed west
without even leaving a note.
I've placed an ad under 'Missing Hands':
Please come back.
It doesn't.

The other one wallows in chocolates
pining away for its mate.
It gorges itself obscenely.
The fingernails turn blue.
It's crusted with mustard and pudding
and refuses to take a bath.
It can't remember its name.
I tell it to go away.
It doesn't.

One would raise a fist to fate if
someone would give a hand while
the other sashays on Main Street
picking up pennies for handstands.

Hanky Panky

When all the smells have been scoured out,
bird song and thunder stilled,
zucchini stapled to their stakes,
cows set in self-cleaning cells,
passion and pissedness curtailed—
how, then, will women without handkerchiefs decide
at moments when desire and need collide?
How, without slanted slow aside,
will they then daub a tear—
no violet voile to veil a brow, reveal
no proxy for the sweet possession they can drop?

How, when a clock contains libraries,
a pill box grief and fear,
will boys without a hanky,
unendowed,
address the ritual moment—
she, despite curtailment, damp-cheeked,
awaiting what he's kept until just now—
a virgin handkerchief.

In the back seat of a flattop engine Ford,
I sobbed my way through the shoulder of his
button-down
oxford cloth
shirt—
he the man who'd later break my life.
Go ahead and cry, he mumbled,
pinning my shoulders back so he could get a look—
those Aryan eyes
that silenced birds
and brought Persephone under—
It's wash and wear.

How, without hankies, will our daughters know

never to trust a man who proffers wash and wear
or is too little moved
when violet voile brushed against brow
reveals and veils
virginity?

Giving Myself Away

You softly swallow my
pride
and wipe
your mouth
on my sleeve.

Stunned to see me
gone,
I read
your garments
for signs:

What's to become of
me
folded
in your hand
like an empty fortune
cookie?

Mother

Summer: Dancing with a Bur Oak

It's summer. Through the window, I see 520 pounds of wood, 2,867,952 oak leaves in various stages of development, 6,987,662 gallons of water, 262 pounds of bark. These are not random guests invited by general announcement to a meeting without purpose. They compose a majestic bur oak, a dynamic living organism. It inclines its every fiber and every ounce of energy toward the augmentation and multiplicity, the greater glory, of oaks.

In the ground beneath me, root fingers stretch and extend, hunting water and minerals to transform into the oakness of this tree, into the fruitfulness that will ensure more oaks. New leaves stretch out, their growing edges driving water, nutrients, and sunlight to the purpose of oakness.

In about four months, this oak will bend its energies to the possibility of new oaks growing. If the weather holds, if the tree finds enough water, enough minerals in the earth and sun to support the extension of life outside itself, the tree will put forth an abundance of acorns: enough for the resident squirrels, enough to rot and make the earth more fruitful, enough to ensure a few new oak shoots in the yard next spring.

In a season of extreme drought, acorns unripe and out of season pummeled us for days. Their clatter sounded the alarm, putting music to our unspoken desperation at the possibility of water dearth. The leaves came down, still green yet dry. Acorn children were sacrificed in these dire circumstances. The tree survived another season.

The oak aggressively promotes the goals of oakness over the goals of other life forms—squirrels, beetles, viruses, fungi. They unwittingly intend to use the oak's living body to grow and further their own mission. But in its fruitful expansion, the oak tree offers to all—even to those who would harm it—the food and shelter that advances life itself.

The oak breathes my breath. I inhale its exhale. The air we breathe is the air you are now breathing. This book may be a remnant of my bur oak's cousin. In the whirl and pause of grateful joy, we share the dance of living, growing, changing, dying to live.

For Indian Jenny from Ken Kesey's *Sometimes a Great Notion*

My house is morning mouthed
Dank and thick to the walls
Animal-scented, sour

Closets hold droppings and bones
Corners harbor bugs
Behind the plaster: molds

Black eyed and toothless,
My house gapes for rain
To loosen the crusty floor.

Dawn spills over the clutter
Loosens the wallpaper
Crouches under chairs.

Behold how light trembles
Water in broken glass:
Rainbows adorn my all.

The Artist at Her Work

An iron chain fastened one end
to post
the other
to capuchin monkey
who

simulates her descendent
Gertrude Stein and acts
as though there is no use
for a center
who

becomes more
than laboratory subject
becomes more than
207 consecutive
problems with stick and banana
when

ignoring the stick
she makes a canvas of the
laboratory floor
and

hovers out geometric shapes
achieving

the effect of

roughly

Mondrian.

Family Heirlooms

In spring I wash the quilts,
invite the sun,
lay out the linens fresh
as blank pages.

Staccato stitches marching
single file
hem in the breath. Your
words unravel.

Keep these, you said,
and then
I've no one else.

New pictures have been hung,
the rooms are clean.
After how many years
is the heart calm?

I've planted zinnias by
the window wall.
Your things are put away,
the trunks are closed.

But when the polished lights
of day are gone,
I hear the scratching in
an attic room
where linens swaddle what
I won't recall.

Pulling Sheets

When our marriage was young,
our pockets empty,
we'd take our love-worn
sheets to the laundromat
in a willow basket that,
later, would hold our son.

Back then
sheets were woven of fibers
that grew in the field, percale
and worsted cotton, and always
the question of wrinkles.

At the end
of the drying cycle, we'd grasp each end
of a sheet, pleat it in our hands and
pull, pull to his German
rhythm, and on my side,
to the Greek. Our eyes locked,

we straightened
the wrinkles, never
pulling so hard—not until
much later—as to
risk that the sheet
would
tear.

Contempt: A Parable

After gulping bird song, thunder,
laughter,
applause,
growl,
footfall,
rock clatter,
the beast surveyed his earth.

All mouths opened,
silent clams, and
even the rain fell
soundless.

The beast said,
It is good.

His hunger turned abruptly
on the vibration of his words,
the grumbling of his body.

Thus (for he was thorough)
he swallowed up himself
to perfect the universe.

Only the eyes remained:
black holes in space
reproaching the silent world,
finding it flawed, grotesque
in its utter
perfected
silence.

Woman's Day

We meet in telephone wires
Stretched between books and husbands
Children potatoes songs
Diapers groceries fevers.

The din of the man's need
Collapsed in his name on a door
Evaporating in whiskey:
It's so loud I can barely hear you.

We quiet too many children
Blooming between our legs
Lick them clean again, again.
At dawn we awake, exhausted.

Our hungers, ghosts in the bone
Curdle milk in the breast.
We are the starving children
Searching for dead mothers.

In another time
I would have stolen your bread.
My need tugs at the skirt
Refuses to cover its head.

In another time
I would have cradled your head
Sung you a lullaby
Of sparrows and magic ships.

You, with your Indian heart
The laugh that begins in the fingers
You've grown as big as a mountain

Beautiful in your bones.
Do you hear that distant moan?
It explodes in my head like a siren.
Our dead mothers are calling.
We are your daughters, I answer.

How the Patriarchy Lost Me

When I found the doors
Of my red pickup truck
Ajar
Phone gone
Laptop case empty
Dead silence
Seemed in order

And me having gone
So proud on the arm of
A man
Of means
Rolex, Armani,
Me golden
With life in thrall

And he so proud
Promising protection
From men
With trucks

Like mine.

Seduction by Piano

The piano in my garage
        amazes night robbers
        lured by the shimmer of hubcaps
        sweet scent of gasoline.

Its ivory, rubbed and worn
        by one hundred years of hands,
        does not require their touch.

They search for removable parts and find none.
They consider renting a dolly and give it up.

At last, I hear them plucking out a few bars of
        Moonlight Sonata,
        clumsy and innocent in the dark.

The notes glide over back yards,
        porch swings, skateboards,
        bikes left unlocked.

In the distance, a dog barks.
Cats mate on rooftops.

The slow and labored music
        drifts into my bed

        steals away

        my
        silence.

Garden Poem: Anatomy of My Mother

She drifts on waves of silver mandolins,
a floating Roman banquet in her sigh.
It is too much, I say, hiding my mouth.
It cannot be, I say, clenching my teeth.

She feeds me silver fishes:
they divide,
lay yellow eggs inside my shaking fingers.
I hold the knife, I say, touching her feet.

The blade dissolves in mist
she comes up silver
pearl in the eye
and glides through eels in shadow.
She is more white than snakes in arteries.

I hold her.

I swim in her.

I am horrified holding her.

She breaks into my mirror.

Bequest

It's a tear in the curtain, a hole in the architecture
transformed to window. Through it you view
what her eyes saw—the judgment, fear, the love.
Faces, hard eyes, purple of lilacs, tunnel through
where she numbers her life in folders
not to cause you any trouble.
The pillow, worn and deep,
where she lay slow, unintended,
apple half eaten, coffee cups unwashed.
Her tools—the loom, sewing machine, such scraps
left. Flowers unpicked.
Or did she pick the roses, wash the cups,
alight in all your senses
so that never again, no, never
will you see through any eye you knew
before you were alloyed,
invaded in her vessel.

In the Pediatric Ward

In this forest of tubes and bottles,
children wander in sleep.
A dying bird drops
from the corner of my eye.
The night nurse floats through paths
tending the rooted tubes,
weighing the pause between breaths.
In the dark, a man's voice
stuns like a hunter's gun.
We wait for dawn.

Last night we cried—four worn children
facing their walls, and I,
handing out animal crackers.
Willow's bones are flaking.
John's eye refuses light.
Paige's ears close up and
something is eating the soft parts of
Adam's knee.
We know these things and we cry.

The children force the beds to do acrobatic tricks.
They've decorated the sheets with urine, gum, and ice cream.
Shrieking, they dribble gravy: Collages bloom on the floor.
They glue flies to the walls, punch holes in dolls and blankets.
The children are not civilized, and the women have left off their makeup.

After the baths, the doctors
visit their explanations
upon the numbered beds.
They know about bones, eyes, ears,
for they've inspected the bodies.
They neither laugh nor cry.
We humor them, for we see
that their suits are too tight,

their shoes pinch,
and they've had little sleep.
But at three in the morning,
Adam and Willow whimper,
aquarium gurgles
IV fluid drips
vibrators hum
a dying bird falls
and the night nurse's thighs
rub, rub in the hall.

Magenta Bike

It isn't wholehearted, this spare
Sears model special
Lacking chrome and reflectors.

It isn't that Blue Huffy
That made your eyes shed diamonds
Your face electric with wonder
Last year on your seventh birthday.
This is homespun, humble.

I don't think they'll steal this one,
You say, counting your shoelaces,
Glancing up at magenta.

Making Things: For My Son

You can make anything out of anything.
Today I made a grasshopper out of a single palm leaf
As mother made a dress from a ball of yarn
As the men down the street are making a wall out of mud.

I've made a bed out of leaves
And bread from flour, water and yeast,
As a bee makes honey from a flower's sweetness
And a child makes a map of the world in crayon

As you make a fire in my heart with a sigh.

Taking Care of Each Other

Does not a marriage make.
I'm weeding the walled garden,
Planning the winter's take
And give—mulberries for jam,
You at the table, your body
Worn from simple labor.
T.V. and lovemaking after,
Enough for the night, for the week.
My body compresses to comfort.

I'm arranging the flowers to please you.
It is not so hard to live without
Worries of feeding the children.
No children. Worries abridged
To the weekend entertainment:
A movie, friends over, tennis,
Reading, a concert, a nap?
My body aches for purpose.
My mind wanders to purpose.

Reduced to self-indulgence,
I pick at the nuance of words.
What did you mean when you turned
To the right and lowered your head?
How does this flick of a wrist
Relate to this turn of the table?
You grieve with old irritation:
Why is it never enough?

I wilt like a leaf under salad
Reclining precise, ornamental.
I am a feast for the planet,
A being that wants to be used.
You're a banquet that wants to be eaten,
To become something bigger than we.
It is not enough, my darling,
To take care of each other
For keeps.

Eco Logos

Just now, in one of those
stretched
out
kitchen moments,
Unto the Seventh Generation
comes down to
washing
the blue glass Shirley Temple pitcher
the one with the faded dimpled child face
the one my son's grandmother
and maybe your grandmother,
when she was a girl
in a sailor dress at breakfast,
used for milk she poured
into her cereal bowl,
the light streaming in a kitchen window
opened by Vermeer.

All this, of course, in the Age of Progress
the age of charmed frogs and pigtail pullers
willing
to fight
the Big War just
to earn
their way to a home where a girl
in a sailor dress
would be forever
pouring
milk
out of a blue glass pitcher.

Or in my mother-in-law's case
the Age of Liberation—
winsome gals
swallowing unspeakable

demands
in typing pools
packing houses
sweatshops
just
to earn a home where
the faded dimpled child
could pour milk forever
out of the pitcher.

This pitcher
the one my mother-in-law gave me
thirty years ago
standing
in the shaft of light in her kitchen
one of those
slow
long
moments between women
yoked
by love of things
of home.

This same blue pitcher in my hand
nested
in the linen towel
scattered with wildflowers
embroidered by
who knows whose grandmother cast off
to the Salvation Army
(time finally reduced to a coil of demands—
interminable wailing of things—
perpetual washing and sorting)
finally abandoned.

In this wildflower bouquet
rejected

into my hands
rests a dimpled child in the sunlight
blue glass by the kitchen window
opened
by Vermeer
pouring,
forever pouring,
unto the seventh generation.

Crone

Autumn: Bur Oak Agonistes

The suckers mortgage the tree's future, says the tree trimmer, scowling. *They ransack its pension, draw on its capital.* I see the suckers as poor cousins clamoring for life, proliferating in a system under stress. They are the raucous rants of abused children, the flattened gaze of drug addicts, the supplications of the homeless. The trimmer inexplicably removes one of the tree's great branches. *It was blocking your neighbor's view,* he says.

I call an arborist. *Leave the suckers*, he tells me. *If you remove them and leave the cause of stress, the suckers will grow back.* His gaze stops at the wound left by the tree trimmer. *The branch was cut too close to the trunk*, he says. We paint the wound black, the color of mourning.

All summer, the oak heals wounds inflicted by squirrels, woodpeckers, ants. It catches the wind and shakes off mites and molds. It reaches higher than the houses to find sunlight. Its shadow makes the earth beneath it inhospitable to other sun seekers. It cracks foundations in search of water and minerals.

A family of squirrels marks a hole in the tree's blackened wound as their doorway and moves in. The following year, the squirrels are evicted by a family of raccoons. The mother raccoon suns herself on a high branch. She brings food to the babies who whimper inside their bur oak home. Year after year, a succession of squirrel families competes for the prime real estate that is the tree's hollow core. One summer day, a squirrel is writhing under the tree, stung and bloated. Above, a swarm of bees has claimed the oak's open heart. I watch the buzzing energy leaving the tree to pollinate the earth, coming home to the cathedral of honeycombs inside the oak.

When my neighbor builds a patio near the base of the oak, the earth lies open, the oak tree's roots broken and exposed. It is the season when beetles seek sap in open wounds. The following spring, the oak's green leaves begin to fall. By mid-summer, the tip of the biggest branch is naked. I lean against the tree and weep.

If the tree's brief relationship with beetles and oak wilt fungus ravaged its core, the tree will abandon its mission of oakness to become compost for the flowers it now shades. I wait for another season. The tree and I sway to the beat of the breathing, continually transforming earth, dying our living, living our dying.

A Panegyric for Violet Crane

Every woman in her sixties
who throws back her head
and cackles at cops and bankers
is named Violet Crane.

And all the girls in plaid shirts
driving fast cars in the desert
wear Violet's eyes.

In my hunt for a fitting mother
I have stalked unruly women
'til they swarmed, kaleidoscopic,
in dragonfly compound visions.

I have startled to see them enter
through all my faceted prisms:
a hundred blooming Violets,
bare-breasted, furry-legged,
picking pears from a mutant vine
whose roots grow deep in their bellies.

They wink while I wait for my supper
dropping pears to me just out of reach.
If I reach for their feet, they vanish
and I never see them again
unless I follow.

I have come to know their ways.
They do not hide behind their fingers.
They do not sit back in their chairs.
They eat standing up.

Once, by the dream of a river
I met a woman who tended

her garden of crystals, who camped
in a rainbow tent in the desert.
I asked if her name was Violet.
When she threw back her head, her laughter
tugged at the roots in my belly.
She pronounced my ways unruly.
She said, *If the name fits, wear it.*

Rebecca West Defines Female and Male Sensibility

Women and men? asks Rebecca West
Idiots and lunatics, present and past.

Idio stands self-stuck, small and alone
Endangers the whole while attending to one
Distracted by color, manner, or style
She obsesses on singular senseless travail.

Luna sees moonlit horizon afar
Counts stars, measures eons—forgets where you are
Scout or protector, he scans for the foe:
If outliers wander, he will lay them low.

Idiots and lunatics, women and men
Chaotic policy, unfinished plan
Married, they struggle, yin versus yang
Seeing each other as thoughtless, insane.

Both in one person? Sanity sweet.
Each side in balance, a comfort complete.

Accoutrements

Epaulets, crowns, accoutrements
Armor of station, age or place—
Slantwise, the wearer pays the price
With practiced show of sentiment.

More attribute than stripes or stars
Are scars, a tangle in the brow
As in your face, the one I know
Unarmed, yet daunted, raw, and fair.

Reptiles, unwrinkled, shed the skin:
An uncreased face shows snake within.

Obituary of a Man Who Kissed Me

Is it you they call beloved father...brother...
Passed away peacefully surrounded by...

The meeting finished, you surrounded me,
Turned me to face you, bent to hold and taste

Is it your name in brass beside this bench
In memory of...he shared with...all he touched...

You touched my face, exploring, eloquent
Smelling of urgency, we left us there.

Eternal be your memory, beloved,
Written in brass and stone, abstracts and deeds

And on my lips, my mouth, nape of my neck.

Epithanatos: On the Death of My Father

If there is fault, it's vague and
       fleeting dusk.

Shrugging,
we watched the limp
       days compress, crushed
like soiled sheets on
       the feeble sky.

The hoarse silence that dipped
       and skimmed the walls
was nothing more than sighing,
       we agreed.

We did not know, 'til night,
       abruptly falling,
heavily pressed its weight on
       the jammed door:

Faint sounds, the block and
       reach of scant breath,
then silence, thick as incense.

Darkness wrapped
       its wings around the broken,
       humbled house.

We bowed to share the silence,
       count a pause,
and kiss the barren woman's
       progeny.

Only after dawn did we
       slant our eyes,
deny, accept, condemn, acquit
       the blindness

       and blame it on
       the briefness of the dusk.

A Crown for My Mother

Because we could not afford a crown
he pulled six molars and left
gums ragged, bleeding, you dazed
yet proud to live in a country
that offered the hope of crowns.
You still had the fronts, so you
could pass for a proper woman.

Until you ate.
Gnawing in front, you exposed
yourself as imposter; no queen
would chew like that
and I, the princess,
found you uncouth
agreed with my brother, the prince,
you should close your mouth, should
eat more slowly, should chew your
food in the back.
You learned to cover your mouth.
You learned to avoid chewing.

How many times I left
, the table, the guests unaware,
the candles still burning,
to see you sink over the drain and
retch retch retch retch
reach for the Gelusil
gnaw chalky aluminum chunks,
grotesque in the front of your mouth.
How many times I returned
to the table, your ulcer in my stomach.

Bridges, too late, would do
for a now impossible crown.
But you outlived your bridges.

Aluminum clogged your brain.
Gelusil drained your mind.
You outlived your wish to die.
We kept you alive for years
on a nursing home pre-chewed diet.
You hoarded food in the cavity
that would have held a crown.
You chewed for hours, fixing
the choice: to spit or swallow.

Without a crown you kept
that final dignity.

Neptune Rising

It's the inconvenience of losing the touchpoints
as the planet's rising erases them
and you find yourself smiling at ground squirrels,
forgetting to sign checks.
What will come of this?
A bag lady future after
a life making lists,
dressing up for the neighbors?

It's the good vibes I'm after,
the being plugged in
things never looked so good
polished surfaces gleaming.
Yet surfaces melt like fudge
and Einstein's elegant abstraction
comes round here in my bedroom
on a clock with no face.

I saw a man push his fingers
into a woman's belly
and pull out a bloody mass
while she discusssed the weather.
I was once eight inches tall.
When he wiped up, he left no scar,
but the incision he made is permanent,
recorded in my neurons.
I was once in my mother's belly.

I want an explanation:
blood capsules under his fingernails,
chicken livers up his sleeve.
Instead, I see her skin dimple
when his fingers aren't quite touching.
I was before I had fingers.

What energy extracts mass
Where the where is the where I was?

The Mathematics of Snow

Round predicates ring
    though this bauble breaks.

Line remains shortest distance
    between two shifting points.

I am as near death
    as any living thing.

And this snow is now
    falling between two points.

The path, in retrospect,
    can be plotted by a fool.

Yet snow falls beyond measure
    of probability.

The secret of angles and lines
    is touched in the Sistine Chapel.

This snow is as near the hand
    as any falling thing.

Biomechanica

One out of ten is composed of the parts of others you've known.
If I blow the stardust of love in your face, this one scatters.

One out of ten knew you in the womb before there was body.
If I take a sword to your marrow, it will not notice.

One out of ten is an error an ancestor made in battle.
If a butterfly passes nearby, the offense is unbearable.

One out of ten is hitching a ride, which confuses the others.
If I squeeze that one hard, it transforms and may fuse to the rest.

One out of ten fails to notice the ones who have never been noticed.
These find a way to remain, and you may not notice.

One out of ten is the fixer, the keeper of rhythms and currents.
If a bulge or a strain fouls the flows, the alarm will be sounded.

One out of ten is so foreign the others would blanch if they knew it.
If a poem or reed should point, there may be revolution.

One out of ten is convinced it's alone and considers this nonsense.
If you should attempt to debate, it would tear you to pieces.

One out of ten seduces the loins to demand satisfaction.
If this one should win, some may start their own journey.

One out of ten is content that its millions have stayed for a moment.
When they scatter, the fragrance of love is left in the children.

Hymn to the Hyrax

The tree hyrax, which is half rabbit and half rat in appearance, but whose internal organs show it to be more closely related to the elephant, is quickly approaching extinction. Sixty-two of the sixty-five tree hyraxes in captivity at the San Diego Zoo have died of ulcers and a worm parasite; large numbers have died of the same causes in their native habitat in Asia and Africa.

A bag of skin confused
Trunk and tusks undescended
Camouflage whiskers in motion
Attuned to dead-end evolution.

Chant *om* oh sweet rat-faced compadre
Turn your snout toward the sun of a far day
Let acids etch art on the bastions
Of painfully narrow intestines.

To the worms, you're a landscape, a wonder,
And the zoo keeper tallies your number
While you gently incline toward Valhalla:
A species too subtle to wallow.

Reconciliation

Winter: Compost and Resurrection

The mite in my compost heap, the fly circling my head, is searching for growth and answers.

I would say to the mite, the fly, to the child coming after me: *Your part is essential in the drama of transforming waste into life. Play your part with grace.* I would warn: *Be careful of too much order, especially if it makes you feel mighty, immortal. The earth can't transform a platoon, so don't fall into step. Don't let chaos seduce you, either. Don't let it break down the scaffold you raise for your next evolution. Honor what you eat as you know you will be eaten.*

You are the most important mite in the universe, I would say, *and you are completely without worth. You are the speck on the butterfly's wing in Brazil, the very butterfly whose movement changes the weather in Kansas. Here is the key: Both your suffering and your joy are necessary. Both your destruction and growth are needed. Without your birth and death the universe could not continue.*

When I learned about Christ's passion—the crown of thorns, the blood running down his cheek—I could smell his sweat, feel his body soiled with fear, trembling in outrageous pain. I saw the mites and viruses take life where the thorns broke his skin. His face radiated peace, and in his gaze I understood He would soon return his being to the life source. He would return His body to the earth so flowers and vegetables could grow. His body would yield the fruits we eat, and in eating we would remember.

The flower, in its moment of passion, its day of glory, touches my soul with its loveliness. I go away fed by it, nurtured by beauty that grows on the compost heap. I marvel and know this may be the cousin of the flower I shall become when it is my turn to return my body to the glorious Mother.

The mystery of turning body into sunflower, sunflower to earth, then perhaps into a tree in which a squirrel builds its nest, a tree that once grew in my garden and warmed my spirit: This is the final mystery. The shared breath and the transformation of waste to glory is all, and all is becoming. I incline my every cell, surrender my every fiber to becoming the compost that serves this so large plan.

Holy Trinity: Maiden, Mother, Crone

The Crone
Here is my home, a rock bottom comfort.
Here is your knowing, your coming to terms.

I'll hold you and lull you to sleep lately severed.
Hold you to the truth of the lump in your throat.

How dare they bind wounds with their supple suggestions.
How dare they hide truth with their adaptive smiles.

Hopeless his name, the proud interloper
The barren begetter who's ravaged my seeds.

Hopeless his name, insatiable claimer
Marking out borders, depleting my bounty.

Hopeless his name, perfumed undertaker
Denying his death and defiling my peace.

My own, my girl child, my song is your succor.
Here where your hopelessness lately has dwelt.

The Maiden
I hear a crone in the thrum of my temples,
Catch her at sunset, a dark wind beyond me.

Thoughts pass like fireflies, I meet them in passing.
My valleys are shallow, my silences brief.

My body is restless, as bread quickly rising.
My arms twine a river, my hands wind a stream.

The twist of a vine in my legs forms a helix.
The life code is written in my belly's seams.

Awakened, I see me displayed like a carcass
Astride pinkest bunting that mimics my skin.

How am I naked?

Why are they leering?

Where can I turn from these slabs of concrete?

I hear you, old woman, as if through a dark wind
Your words are a murmur I catch in a dream.

The Mother
An old woman passes, a bag lady presence
She searches their garbage for something to eat.

Her hopelessness beckons, but I will not answer.
I cannot reach out to her perilous shadow.

Parade float, pink bunting, glides on the cold street.
A death march display of a woman who's naked.

I have called her shameless, deserving their leering.
Now I fear for her taking, bewail her abandon.

I tell her beware the beguiling pretender.
Cover your sex, child, and lock up your dreams.

Beware naked flesh and the murmur of knowing.
Keep nothing to savor, have nothing to fear.

I'm dressed to the teeth, I have straightened my stockings.
I lock up the house and I wander the streets.

Reconciliation
Deep in the bowels of my valleys, old woman,
I find you awakened from eons of sleep.

I listen for knowing, a mooring in storm winds.
I listen for me in the heart of your calling.

A woman who's passing wraps me in a blanket.
I see her exhausted, I see her afraid.

I reach for her power, you pull her beside you.
We stand in the street by some empty parade.

We're choosing our path, step by step, through the wasteland.
We wonder in passing just whose are these streets.

From the blood of our moontimes a lullaby beckons.
It's caught in my throat, a keening serene.

It enters the spaces between toes and fingers.

She's calling, I'm singing, a new Ave Eva.

We float Ave Eva surprised by our breathing.

We fly Ave Eva. Awakening. Clean.

About the Author

Tess Galati is a Greek immigrant who grew up in Iowa. At seventeen, she was sent back to "the old country" to be appropriately groomed and correctly married. She returned to the U.S., triumphant and unmarried, picked up a passel of scholarships and completed a doctoral degree. Tess has been a mother once, wife twice, waitress briefly, and college professor way  too long. She has given all she has to the art of teaching. For four decades, Tess's work as a writing consultant in corporate America stimulated her mind and fed her family. Having swept away most of the encumbrances in her life, Tess now writes, paints, tends her bees, plays with her grandchildren, entertains her guests, travels, gardens, and cooks on impulse and without ambition.

About the Icon

This icon, written in the Byzantine tradition, symbolizes the core connection and conflict of maiden, mother, and crone—the three phases a woman must enter and integrate in order to become whole.

In the icon, the staff transforms into the double helix of DNA, symbolizing the tree of life. The Maiden points to the staff, unconsciously indicating that her body is the vessel that creates life. The Mother points to the egg and holds the staff like a javelin, as though she's willing to throw it rather than have the Maiden be damaged by its power. The Crone, who is closest to wisdom and death, holds the staff easily and, with her right hand, supports the Mother.

The Mother looks to the past, to community as it has been, while the Crone looks to the future, to the growing branches of the tree of life. The Maiden innocently looks straight ahead. Each woman also has an eye of inner knowing, or third eye, in the center of her forehead. The Maiden's is covered by a pearl, a symbol of innocence. The Mother's is barely visible, for she is more conscious of community and family than of inner truths. The Crone's third eye is prominent. Her face is also marked by tear lines and a ridge over the eyebrows known as the prophet's brow. These are signs of her suffering and her wisdom.

The Maiden is fittingly naked, having not yet learned the dangers of naked vulnerability. The colors of the mother's and crone's garments, ranging from dark red to iridescent violet, parallel the gradation of colors from the lowest to the highest chakra in Eastern philosophy, which is exactly the same gradation found in Byzantine iconography. The Mother's wimple forms a keyhole, symbolizing the fact that we come through the mother.

Byzantine icons tell archetypal stories that explain and direct the life of the soul. They are meant to be read for meaning, not admired for form. As you read this icon and the words in this book, you follow one woman's soul in its journey toward personal integration and universal celebration.

Made in the USA
Columbia, SC
30 March 2022

58340402R00133